RATTLESNAKES

BY: ERIC ETHAN

Gareth Stevens Publishing
A WORLD ALMANAC EDUCATION GROUP COMPANY

Please visit our web site at: www.garethstevens.com
For a free color catalog describing Gareth Stevens' list of high-quality books
and multimedia programs, call 1-800-542-2595 (USA) or 1-800-461-9120 (Canada).
Gareth Stevens Publishing's Fax: (414) 332-3567.

Library of Congress Cataloging-in-Publication Data

Ethan, Eric.
    Rattlesnakes / by Eric Ethan.
       p. cm. — (Fangs! an imagination library series)
    Includes index.
    Summary: Describes what rattlesnakes look like, what they eat,
where they can be found, how they defend themselves, the danger
from their bites, and the outlook for their future.
    ISBN 0-8368-1431-2 (lib. bdg.)
    1. Rattlesnakes—Juvenile literature. [1. Rattlesnakes.
2. Poisonous snakes. 3. Snakes.] I. Title. II. Series:
Ethan, Eric. Fangs! an imagination library series.
QL666.O69E86 1995
597.96—dc20   95-19264

Published in 1995 by:
Gareth Stevens Publishing
A World Almanac Education Group Company
330 West Olive Street, Suite 100
Milwaukee, WI 53212 USA

Original text: Eric Ethan
Series design: Shari Tikus
Cover design: Karen Knutson
Photo credits: All photos © Joe McDonald except Page 17 © J. H. Carmichael

Printed in the United States of America

6 7 8 9 10 11 12 05 04 03 02 01

TABLE OF CONTENTS

WHAT ARE RATTLESNAKES?

Rattlesnakes are the most common poisonous snake in the United States and Canada. Over twenty-five species have been found. The three most common rattlesnakes are the timber rattlesnake, western rattlesnake, and massasauga. The first part of the scientific name for all rattlesnakes is *Crotalus* (KRO ta less) or *Sistrurus* (SIS trur es). Both of these words mean rattle-tail.

A diamondback rattlesnake about to strike.

WHAT DO THEY LOOK LIKE?

Every rattlesnake has a tail rattle. When one is angry its tail shakes making a buzzing or hissing sound. Each time a rattlesnake sheds its skin the rattle gets longer. In adults the rattle can reach 2 inches (5 cm) or more. All snakes must shed their skin to grow. First the old skin becomes dry and thin. A new skin forms on the snake and then it crawls out of its old one.

The largest Rattlesnakes grow to 35-65 inches (90-165 cm). The massasauga reaches half that, 18-30 inches (45-135 cm). Rattlesnakes have flat wide heads shaped like a triangle and a slender body. Their bodies are covered by flat, tough plates called scales. As you can see in this book, rattlesnakes come in many different colors and patterns.

This mottled rock rattlesnake's head is shaped like a triangle.

WHERE ARE THEY FOUND?

Rattlesnakes can be found in almost every state and in parts of southern Canada. They live in forests and rocky areas of North America. They also live in deserts. Some eastern diamondback rattlesnakes live in the wet areas of the southeast, but most rattlesnakes avoid going in the water.

In cold areas rattlesnakes **hibernate** in dens. Sometimes large numbers of rattlesnakes hibernate together. These dens can be found on rocky ledges or holes in the ground.

When the sun is out rattlesnakes like to warm themselves. Snakes are cold blooded. This means they are only as warm as the air around them unless they can find a place to sun themselves.

This is a timber rattlesnake. It is found in many parts of the United States.

SENSES AND HUNTING

Scientists believe snakes cannot hear well. And they cannot see very far. But rattlesnakes are **predators**. This means they must eat other animals to stay alive. How do rattlesnakes find their prey?

Rattlesnakes use their tongues to know what is near them. Each time the tongue flicks out of a snake's mouth it takes a sample of the air and ground. In the rattlesnake's mouth the **Jacobson's organ analyzes** what the tongue picks up. This tells the rattlesnake what is around it.

A diamondback rattlesnake showing its tongue.

Rattlesnakes have small pits between their eyes and nose. These are called **loreal pits**. They allow the snake to detect warm prey even at night.

Some rattlesnakes hunt at night. Most of these ambush their prey which means the snake sits and waits in one place until its tongue and pits tell it prey is close.

In warmer areas rattlesnakes may hunt during the day. Some of them will track prey and sneak up on it before striking.

*Can you see the loreal pits on
this sidewinder rattlesnake?*

WHAT DO THEY EAT?

Rattlesnakes eat small **mammals** like rats and mice.   They also eat birds, lizards, and frogs. Rattlesnakes usually strike and let go. Their **venom** works quickly and their prey does not go far. But if they attack birds they hold on. Birds can fly too far after being bitten for the snake to find again.

Snakes always swallow their prey head first. This makes it easier to swallow. Snake's mouths can open very wide. This allows rattlesnakes to kill and swallow larger prey like rabbits. A rattlesnakes has a breathing tube that goes all the way to the front of its mouth. This allows it to swallow large prey without choking.

This timber rattlesnake has caught a flying squirrel.

SELF-DEFENSE

Most rattlesnakes have very strong venom. They have few enemies except humans. If they can, rattlesnakes will move away from danger. They do not want to waste venom on animals they cannot eat.

Some species of rattlesnakes are aggressive. This means they will attack rather than move away from danger. The sound of a rattlesnake's tail is an important warning to move away.

Camouflage is the rattlesnake's best defense. It can be difficult to see one when it is laying quietly on the ground.

The body of this banded rock rattler is well camouflaged.

RATTLESNAKE BITES

A rattlesnake uses its tail rattle as a warning. If it does bite it injects venom through its fangs. Fangs are very sharp hollow teeth. In fully grown rattlesnakes, the fangs are about 1/2 inch long (1.3 cm). The snake's fangs are folded back to the top of its mouth when not in use.

Rattlesnake venom is very strong and can easily kill an adult human. Doctors will give people bitten by rattlesnakes **antivenin** to help them. Scientists use the rattlesnake's own venom to make antivenin.

The fang and venom of a diamondback rattlesnake.

UNUSUAL FACTS

In the wild, rattlesnakes live about ten to fifteen years. But if they are well taken care of in zoos, they can live to thirty years.

Even dead rattlesnakes can be dangerous. In one true case a person was killed when he stepped on the fangs of a dead rattlesnake.

The Hopi Indians of the southwest used to use the western rattlesnake in a special ceremony. During the Hopi Indian snake dance the snakes would be carried in the mouth and hands of dancers.

A rare albino diamondback rattlesnake.

THE FUTURE

In the past people often killed rattlesnakes to get a **bounty**. They thought rattlesnakes were dangerous to people and farm animals. Today people know that rattlesnakes help control pests like rats and mice.

The biggest danger to rattlesnakes today is loss of **habitat**. As land is used for cities and farms snakes lose a place to live. Sometimes the food they eat goes away first and snakes can no longer live there.

Desert rattlesnakes of the southeast live far from most people. They have a safer place to live. In eastern states like New York and New Jersey rattlesnakes have almost disappeared.

GLOSSARY

analyze (AN a lize) - To separate something into its parts to study them.

antivenin (AN tee ve nin) - Medicine that works against the poison in a snakes venom.

bounty (BOUN tee) - A reward for killing an animal.

camouflage (KAM 0 flazh) - Colors or patterns that helps an animal look like the ground around it.

habitat (HAB i tat) - The place where an animal is normally found.

hibernate (HI ber nate) - To spend the winter in a deep sleep.

Jacobson's organ (JAY kob sons OR gan) - A special pouch in a snake's mouth that analyzes what the tongue picks up.

loreal pit (LOR e all) - A small hole near a snake's nose that can see infrared light.

mammal (MAM el) - A warm-blooded animal that has a backbone.

predator (PRED a tor) - An animal that lives by killing and eating other animals.

venom (VE nom) - The poison of snakes.

INDEX

PLACES TO WRITE FOR MORE INFORMATION

American Society of Ichthyologists and Herpetologists
US National Museum
Washington, DC 20560

Copeia
American Society of Herpetologists
34th Street and Girard Avenue
Philadelphia, PA 19104

Herpetologists' League
1041 New Hampshire Street
Lawrence, KS 66044

Herpetological
1041 New Hampshire Street
Lawrence, KS 66044